JAPAN

DUANE R. RUBIN

JAPAN

CUSTOMS AND CULTURE

**Foreword
Takahide
Yamada**
Director
Japan
National
Tourist
Organization

**A TRAVEL
ENJOYMENT
BOOK**

CELESTIAL ARTS
Millbrae, California

Copyright © 1975 by Celestial Arts
231 Adrian Road, Millbrae, California 94030

First Printing, January, 1975
Made in the United States of America

Library of Congress Cataloging in Publication Data

Rubin, Duane R   1931-
    Japan : customs and culture.

    (A Travel enjoyment book)
    1. Japan--Social life and customs--1945-
I. Title.
DS822.5.R8   390'.0952   74-25833
ISBN 0-912310-004-7

Foreword

I am very interested to know and concerned about how our country may be reflected to foreign travellers. In some travel books, facts about Japan are strangely distorted.

When I finished reading this book, I was very happy to find that the Japanese people, our customs, traditions and culture had been described interestingly and correctly. Furthermore, I could not help smiling at the author's humoristic point of view in some places. His way of observing Japan is sometimes unique, and I know that's why this book is interesting and enjoyable.

Mr. Duane R. Rubin has a long travel career background of approximately 21 years: 6 years in two airlines and 15 years in several travel agencies. During the years of 1968 to 1972, he visited Japan 42 times and lived in an apartment near Tokyo for six months. This experience and his knowledge about Japan are condensed effectively in this book.

Through this book you will enjoy a journey in Japan. I wish Mr. Rubin's most interesting book all the success it deserves.

Takahide Yamada
Director, San Francisco Office
Japan National Tourist Organization

Contents

vii

Lovingly and respectfully
dedicated to
Mrs. Kazuko Yashima-Rubin
for her guidance and assistance

JAPAN

Introduction

The idea for this book was born in the mind of the author during an overnight stay at the world famous Fujiya Hotel located in the fairy-tale-like town of Miyanoshita, Japan. This hotel, within the boundary of Hakone National Park, is one of my personal favorites as it affords a chance to relax in the natural hot springs baths and to have a massage in the best Japanese tradition. While relishing the beauty and service of one of the world's finest resort hotels, it occurred to me that the group of American tourists I was managing as tour director was not so comfortable and was not enjoying their stay as they should.

After our visit to the Fujiya Hotel I took great pains to observe tourists of all nationalities as they traveled throughout all the continents and secret Shangri-la's. I became supersensitive to the American and his or her behavior patterns overseas. It became apparent that Americans in a national sense, regardless of ethnic or racial loyalties, were generally not ugly or obnoxious. In most cases where an altercation occurred—an American tourist making unreasonable demands, an embarrassing personal gesture, an argument on politics or religious philosophies, or a supercritical personality in play—the cause was naïveté. In other words, a lack of understanding the traditions, customs and cultures of the land and the people about them. Somehow the travel industry of the United States was failing to properly educate and prepare the traveler to foreign destinations as to what to expect and how to behave in given situations.

Throughout my travels I searched in vain for English language material that could solve these problems efficiently. Instead all I found were the endless volumes of travel guide books consisting of hundreds of pages of reading material devoted mostly to telling the traveler where to stay, where to eat, what to buy, and what to see with a few gloss-over paragraphs on etiquette. The authors of such guide books must be men with nine lives and the fortitude of the Vikings of old to have lived in every hotel they recommend, to have gluttoned themselves in every restaurant they speak about with intimate eloquence or to have experienced the beauty of every sightseeing adventure they expound upon. They must all be in the millionaire category to be such experts on all the things you simply must buy while your luggage gets heavier and your traveler's checks take wing.

As the idea of this book grew in my mind, it was conceived as a way to teach simple travel etiquette in entertaining style, in a short format, thus permitting people to learn as they go and still have the time for fun which is one of the most important ingredients of enjoyable and educational travel experiences.

Since 1953 I had been engaged in the travel industry both as an airline employee and as a travel agent. This occupation required a great deal of travel throughout the world and in 1968 I decided to take something of a sabbatical from the strains and pressures of administration and sales work and start traveling professionally as a tour director. By March of 1970 I had covered close to 2 million miles of mainly international travel and since that time have covered another 400,000 miles at least.

It is the sincere hope and heartfelt wish of the author that each person coming in contact with this book will be able to find something of themselves in the incidents demonstrating what can happen to those not familiar with Japanese customs. Use your imagination; put yourself into the situations and consider how you would act or react.

While the examples may give the indication that I feel all tourists are buffoons stumbling their way through Japan, they are actually intended to enlighten today's travelers in regard to common courtesies, traditions, cultures and customs not normally discussed in travel guide books. This is *not* a guide book and will *not* contain any information as to where to stay, where to eat, where to shop, or even where to go sightseeing. The purpose is to at least attempt to make your trip more comfortable and to aid in your understanding of the different environment you do, or will soon, find yourself in. Without the ability to laugh at ourselves we have little talent for life itself.

The author is a humanitarian seeking to contribute creatively to the future peace of man and the ability to live together in reasonable harmony regardless of ethnic loyalties, racial bloodlines, political philosophies, religious beliefs, lifestyles, class consciousness, hang-ups, addictions, or whatever it takes to set the ego of mankind going in a backward direction.

It is now time for you to sit back and relax, at home, on a plane, or a ship going somewhere, or your first night in a hotel in a foreign land with which you are totally unfamiliar. By the time you reach the end of this book, it is the author's hope that you will have learned a few important facts, had a few good laughs and, most of all, have a feeling of familiarity with customs, traditions and cultures of the land or lands you are or will be visiting.

1

The Big Little Country

Japan can very rightly be called the *Big Little Country*. Known in the Japanese language as *Nippon* or *Nihon*, Japan is an independent state consisting of a chain or islands off the east coast of mainland Asia. It is populated by some 120 million people concentrated mainly on the four principal Islands of Honshu, Kyushu, Shikoku and Hokkaido. Approximately 10 percent of the population lives in Tokyo thus making Tokyo the world's largest city. Translated into English, Tokyo means *Eastern Capital*.

In size, Japan consists of 143,619 square miles, of which only about 16 percent is usable for agriculture, industry and residential areas. Japan being an extremely mountainous country with rugged terrain. By comparison the state of California in the U.S.A. consists of 158,693 square miles with a population of about 20 million people. A few comparative calculations can readily explain the crowded conditions of Japan, the total utilization of every square inch of usable land, the herds of humanity in the metropolitan areas and the official government concern about birth rates and their promotion of birth control.

5

In recent years Japan has become an economic giant and as of 1972 was third in the entire world in terms of gross national product, surpassed only by the United States of America and the Soviet Union in that order. Japan, however, is not rich in natural resources and must depend on the importation of raw materials to support its vast industrial complex. The exportation of Japan's products becomes equally important to its economic strength as within itself Japan is unable to consume even a major portion of its industrial productivity. The myriad of trade agreements and huge investments which Japan has made on an international scale are the country's lifelines.

Japanese recorded history is considered to have begun in the 5th century A.D. at which time Japan began to construct a method of handwriting from the highly developed Chinese culture. Buddhism was introduced to Japan in A.D. 552 and grew to become one of the two principal religions of the country. The other being Shinto which is a cult embracing the worship of nature and ancestors and is common only to Japan. Most Japanese today practice both Shintoism and Buddhism. Their homes usually contain small altars of separate natures, one for Shinto and one for Buddha. Curiously enough a wedding in Japan is usually performed under Shinto rituals and a funeral is usually performed Buddhist style. There are, of course, Japanese who practice only the Shinto faith or the Buddhist faith. Christianity is almost nonexistent in Japan and it is said that less than 5 percent of the population are in any way involved in Christianity. Only at Nagasaki, on the Island of Kyushu, can one find a large Christian influence, Catholic in nature. Protestants exist only in very small numbers throughout the country.

Neither the Shinto faith nor the Buddhist faith have a particular day of worship as is Sunday in the Western world. Japan is, therefore, a seven day a week country with retailers being open for business daily. Large department stores in the metropolitan areas usually close for one day on alternate days of the week, thus one can always find a major department store in operation on any of the seven days. In recent years, however, Japanese offices have adopted the weekend closure custom of the Western world.

Christmas, being Christian, is not a big deal in Japan. New Year's, January 1, is the big holiday and festivities and celebrations extend over a period of several days. The Japanese practice their religious life in a quiet unassuming manner going to temple (in the case of Buddhism) or the shrine (in the case of Shintoism) whenever they so desire. This usually involves a monetary gift to the temple or shrine and a short period of prayer and devotion before the altar.

To provide a complete insight into the two religious philosophies of the Japanese and the many varied sects of their religions is an impossible task. One interesting note, however, is that Buddhism as practiced in Japan is quite different from Buddhism in other parts of the Far East. The Japanese believe that anyone is capable of becoming Buddha and they do not worship the image of Buddha and, in some cases, I have witnessed the destruction of a statue of Buddha as part of the Japanese theater. In other parts of the Far East the religion encompasses the philosophy that there is only one Buddha and that Buddha is worshipped as a deity. Buddhism is considered to be the source of strength by which the Japanese maintain their composure, their patience, their understanding, and their considerate politeness towards each other in their daily lives.

Jimmu Tenno, ruler of Yamato, is considered the founder of the imperial line dating back to 660 B.C., accomplished by invasion by a group of warriors of Manchurian-Korean-Malaysian origin. At this time the aborigines of Japan, the Ainus, were gradually driven northward and now exist in small numbers only on the Island of Hokkaido. The plight of the Ainu in many ways is similar to that of the North American Indian.

The history of Japan for many centuries was anything but peaceful with military feudalism originating in the 9th century A.D. and not eliminated until the 15th century. In following centuries, 17th to the 19th, Japan virtually isolated itself from outside contact. Commodore Perry, U.S. Navy, in the late 19th century, visited the Yokohama harbor in an effort to break the isolation policy and was eventually successful. This long period of isolation is the basic reason that Japanese traditions, customs and cultures are so different from much of the world and have in many ways remained so to the present time.

The Japanese calendar is undoubtedly one of the most confusing of any that have ever been conceived as it is based upon the period of reign of the emperor. The year 1975, for example, is the year 50 of the Showa Era, which is the era covering the reign of Emperor Hirohito who became emperor upon the death of Emperor Taisho on December 25, 1926, which brought to an end the fifteenth year of the Taisho Era and immediately became the first year of the Showa Era. However, era years must also change on the first of January thus exactly six days after the first year of the Showa Era began it became the second year of the Showa Era. Thus there were three era years within a period of one week. The Showa Era is the 230th era in the history of Japan. The business world of Japan today has accepted and uses the same Western style dates along with showing the era year on all official documents, correspondence, etc. The era system has, however, made a tracing of Japanese history and important events an extremely difficult task.

Starting in 1894, Japan became a conquering nation involved in many wars over the land areas of China, Manchuria, Korea, Formosa and others. World War I resulted in the Germans giving possession to the Japanese of German-held islands in the Pacific.

On December 7, 1941, Japan attacked the Hawaiian Islands, then a possession of the United States prior to its statehood days. In the early stages of the war Japan made rapid progress in its conquests. Actually, Japan was too successful as the distances of conquered territory caused logistic problems in maintaining supplies and the turning point in this disastrous war soon came. On August 6, 1945, the United States dropped the atomic bomb on Hiroshima; on August 8, 1945, Russia invaded Manchuria and wiped out the Japanese; and on August 9, 1945, the United States dropped the atomic bomb on Nagasaki. Many war historians feel it was the disaster suffered in Manchuria from the invasion by the USSR that brought the ugly war to a finish and the atomic bombings of Hiroshima and Nagasaki were somewhat incidental.

In September of 1945, U.S. military forces landed in Japan as an occupation force under the leadership of General Douglas MacArthur. War trials were held and punishments to the Japanese leaders, both military and political, were handed down. General MacArthur, however, was successful in his efforts to spare the life of Emperor Hirohito as he felt any moves made toward the Emperor would endanger the morale of the Japanese citizenry who, at the time, considered the Emperor almost a deity. General MacArthur requested that the Emperor publicly announce to the Japanese in a radio address the fact or philosophy that he, the Emperor, was nothing other than another human being, and requested that his fellow Japanese cooperate with the occupation forces to bring about a reconstruction of Japan and a return to peace in the land.

During the period of occupation many reforms were instituted by General MacArthur and a new constitution was adopted in 1947. A land reform was brought into effect which returned the land to the people and brought an end to the dominant landlords in the majority of the country. There presently are very strict regulations as to how much land a Japanese may own, even for agricultural purposes, which amounts to only a few acres. The power of the industrial giants was broken. Freedom of speech, religion, political philosophies and a government operating under the parliamentary system were instituted. Political freedom brought to Japan a proliferation of political parties that has complicated the efficiency of government in recent years. In Japan, the legislative house is called *the diet* and the prime minister is the head of government. He, of course, is always a member of the majority party. Emperor Hirohito still reigns as the emperor of Japan carrying on the imperial line and tradition. His is a position of respect, a tradition that most likely will never be broken.

In 1951, Japan and the United States of America signed a mutual security treaty which, upon proper notice, can be cancelled by either country. Japan has not re-armed herself militarily except to maintain a relatively small national defense force relying on the United States for military support

in the event of a major world conflict. In 1972 the United States returned the island of Okinawa to the Japanese government.

It appears to be the attitude of the Japanese today that General MacArthur's land reform act was the one good thing he did for the country. Otherwise he is pictured as an egotistical military officer who made himself generally unavailable to anyone and in turn created an aura of deification that he had asked Emperor Hirohito to denounce.

There is little indication in Japan today that a disastrous war ever occurred except in Hiroshima with its graphic memorials to the infamous atomic bomb that fell there on August 6, 1945.

Japan is a land of sightseeing delights. Its most outstanding feature geographically is Mt. Fuji, or, in Japanese, Fujiyama. It is incorrect to say Mt. Fujiyama because the Japanese word *yama* means mountain. She is presently a sleeping volcano though small wisps of smoke can sometimes be seen escaping from crevices within her crater. Her last eruption, of which there were 15 of a violent nature, is said to have been in the 14th century. She is a perfect cone in shape and stands alone for the eye to feast on when she sheds her cloudy robes. Fujiyama is considered to be a sacred mountain and it is something of a pilgrimage to the Japanese to make the rugged hike to the top as hundreds do every year. Every source of reference gives her height in feet a little differently but the Japanese tourist guides tell you that Fujiyama is 12,365 feet high. It is very close to her actual height but the story adds to her aura of perfection as they say it is 1,000 feet for each month of the year topped by one foot for each day of the year.

The ancient capital of Japan, Kyoto, is the country's most interesting city by far. It has a population of about 2.5 million people and has been able to retain remnants of its colorful history for centuries. Kyoto was not bombed during World War II in order to preserve the city's historical and cultural treasures. For over 1,000 years Kyoto was the residence of Japan's emperors. It is said that Kyoto is truly representative of old Japan. Among her treasures are more than 600 Shinto shrines and over 1,500 Buddhist temples.

Japan is serenity and madness at the same time. The Japanese are quiet, shy, courteous and polite in their personal relationships. However, on trains, buses, in traffic, crowds and elevators, they are almost brutal. Japan is often referred to as *topsy-turvy country* and you will learn why as you visit this fascinating land.

2

Moshi Moshi

The language of Japan is one of the world's most difficult to read and write. The history of the language dates back to the 5th century when writing taken from the Chinese cultures was brought to Japan.

The Japanese language today is a combination of over 1,800 Chinese characters (*kanji*) in ideograph form complemented by two phonetic alphabets known as *hiragana* and *katakana*. The characters of hiragana and katakana are simpler in form than the kanji characters. Hiragana is used basically to give Japanese its grammar. Katakana is used primarily for the translation of foreign words and names in addition to Japanese proper names. The language can be written and read by the use of any one of these systems, however, Japanese today is a combination of all three systems. Now that you are thoroughly confused, you will be startled to learn that 99.5 percent of the Japanese population is totally literate.

Japanese as a written language is done in different styles of vertical writing and horizontal writing. In the vertical style it is read from top to bottom and from right to left. Japanese written in horizontal style is read from left to right as in the Western style. This style, however, is usually reserved for technical and scientific publications.

Calligraphy, the art of fine writing, is considered a part of the art culture of Japan and is required in Japanese education. The ability to stylize the characters into a picture of sweeping harmony is highly prized and a well-paid profession. You will find the written Japanese to be an integral part of most art work in Japan.

Every visitor to Japan should try to learn a few simple phrases or words to enhance your travel enjoyment. Japanese is a totally phonetic language and it is not difficult to speak. Japanese words when translated into Roman letters, *roma-ji,* are easily pronounced phonetically.

To correctly pronounce a Japanese word one must only learn that the vowel sounds are much the same as in many European languages, especially the Romance languages. The Japanese do not list their vowels in the same order as the Western world but to facilitate your understanding of the vowel sounds we will show you them as they are listed in the English language.

A is pronounced *ah* as in *a*lmond.
E is pronounced *aye* as in *a*men.
I is pronounced *ee* as in b*ea*n.
  Note: Interestingly enough there is no *I* (*eye*) sound in the Japanese language.
O is pronounced *oh* as in g*o.*
U is pronounced *ou* as in m*oo*n.

Japan is not a land of many dialects and the language is pronounced pretty much the same way throughout the country. There is one common vowel sound elimination which is essentially without rule except for the harmony of sound, that is the vowel sound *U.*

An example familiar to us all would be the internationally known Japanese meal *sukiyaki.* In correct Japanese you would say phonetically *sue-key-yah-key.* You will, however, find it pronounced many times as *ski-yah-key.* Both are correct in

usage. There is a district in Tokyo called *Asakusa* which is rather famous for its night life. Phonetically you would say *ah-sah-koo-sah.* It is, however, usually said by the Japanese as *ah-sock-sah.* Another famous area of Tokyo is *Shinjuku* which is always pronounced *shin-joo-koo.*

You may have heard that all Japanese students in recent years have been required to study English in school. This is quite true. However, you will find English is not readily spoken in Japan and when spoken with a Japanese accent is difficult to understand. Many Japanese are also very shy about trying to use what English they know as you will likely be hesitant in your efforts with Japanese.

There have been many stories and jokes about how the Japanese mix up their *R*s and *L*s. Actually, they do not mix them, it is just an accent situation created by the fact that there is no *L* sound in the Japanese language. There is the same situation for *V*, usually pronounced as *B*. Most Japanese syllables end in a vowel sound, thus, they usually add a vowel sound at the end of English words that end in a consonant.

The simple word *table* spoken by a Japanese comes out sounding like *tah-bay-ruh. Vanilla ice cream* is a real grabber as it comes out sounding like *bah-nee-rah eye-soo coo-ree-moo.* A Japanese visitor in San Francisco does not simply say *Post Street,* which is the main street of the Japanese Cultural Center in San Francisco, he would say *Post-o Street-o.* On many occasions while working as a tour director and on departure from Japan by airline, the local guide, who was usually female and Japanese, would say to my group of travelers in her closing remarks: "Prease have a nice fright to Hong Kong."

Counting in Japanese is fun and easy and goes like this:

1 *ichi*   (ee-chee)
2 *ni*   (nee)
3 *san*   (sahn)
4 *shi*   (shee) Since *shi* also means *death,* the word *yon* (yohn) is often substituted.
5 *go*   (goh)

0 *roku*   (roh-koo)
7 *shichi* (shee-chee) Sometimes *nana* (nah-nah) is used as *shichi* is difficult to pronounce in some number combinations.
8 *hachi* (hah-chee)
9 *ku*   (koo)
10 *ju*   (joo)

Into all our lives must come that moment when we need to stop at the nearest gas station. In one of the coming chapters we will have more fun with this situation, but it would be helpful to know that the Japanese word for toilet is *benjo* (ben-joe). In Japanese the prefix *O* or *O-benjo* is more correct. The addition of the *O* merely means honorable toilet. This *O* prefix is quite often used with nouns in the Japanese language. *O-benjo doko desca?* (oh-ben-joe-doh-koh-dehs-kah?), literally translated means "Honorable toilet where is?" or "Where is the honorable toilet?"

Yes and *no* of Japanese is another interesting matter in that you will constantly hear the word *hai* (high) being said over and over again quickly and energetically. That simply means *yes*. There is a Japanese word for *no* and it is *iie* (ee-yeh) but I sincerely doubt that you will ever hear it because the Japanese have a thing about saying *no*. They are optimistic in nature and anything that is a downer just does not fit their personalities. If you were to say to a Japanese hotel clerk in a questioning way, "Did you say I could have a room?" He would very likely answer by saying, "Yes, we are lucky to have all our rooms filled at present time." Never expect to get a *no* answer to any question you put to a Japanese as the reply will always begin with the affirmative.

Now let's learn a few more helpful phrases or words. If you do, you will find the Japanese smiling at you and wanting to be your friend because you have taken the time to learn a little Japanese, indicating a sense of intelligence that they respect a great deal.

Thank you	*Arigato*	(ah-ree-gah-TOH) Emphasize the capital letters
You are welcome	*Do itashimashite*	(DOH ee-tah-shee-mah-shee-tah)
Please	*Dozo*	(DOH-zoh)
Excuse me	*Gomennasai*	(goh-mehn-nah-sahee)
How much?	*Ikura?*	(ee-koo-rah)
Good morning	*Ohayo*	(oh-high-YOH)
Good day (afternoon)	*Konnichiwa*	(kohn-nee-chee-wah)

Note: The above expression is generally used from about 10 a.m. to 3 p.m. after which the following phrase is used.

Good evening	*Konbanwa*	(kohn-bahn-wah)
I do not understand	*Wakarimasen*	(wah-kah-ree-mah-sehn)
Good-bye	*Sayonara*	(sah-YOH-nah-rah)

The study of the Japanese language is fascinating. The artistic kanji really are pictographs in many ways. Space does not permit me to show how they are made but below are the characters for *men* and *women*—for obvious reasons.

MEN   WOMEN

By now you have probably forgotten that this chapter was entitled *Moshi Moshi* and I'm certain you wondered at its meaning. It is simply how you answer the telephone or get someone's attention. It sounds like *mushy mushy*.

3

Got a Yen?

The monetary unit in Japan is the *yen*. In today's world the yen is one of the strongest currencies, but handling it is a little difficult as it is used in such large denominations relative to what most of us are used to. Since this book is not intended to be a guide book, no attempt will be made to go into an explanation of exchange rates for Japanese money.

Paper money is beautifully printed and each denomination is printed on different sizes of paper. There are notes in the following denominations:

¥   100
¥   500
¥   1,000 - the most common bill in use
¥   5,000
¥ 10,000

Coinage is varied, has some peculiarities and some have no Roman markings for identification. Shown on the following page are simple line drawings of the various coins in Japanese yen.

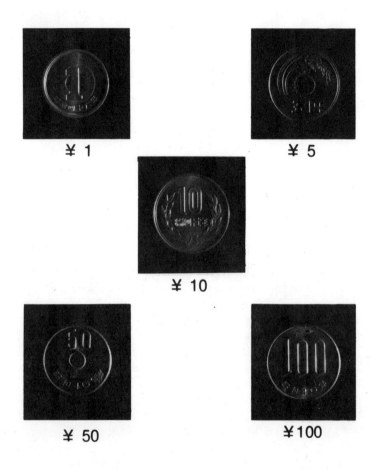

¥ 1 ¥ 5

¥ 10

¥ 50 ¥100

In Japan there is no advantage to going to a bank to change your money and it is best to simply have it done by the hotel cashier. If you go to a bank you will be required to go through reams of paper work and long periods of waiting to get a simple job done.

4

Meeting Manners Matter

Self-respect and respect for their fellow man seems to be the byword of everyday Japanese life. In meeting and greeting each other, the ritual is purely Japanese. It is, in action, beautifully sensitive in many ways. On greeting each other the Japanese do not shake hands. They bow to each other showing graceful respect which brings admiring glances and smiles to the faces of visitors to Japan.

The physical part of greeting each other Japanese style is not simple. The custom of bowing is centuries old and it is within this tradition that stations in life are established. In performance the feet are placed close together and the body motion is from the waist up. The lower a person bows the more humility and respect is indicated to the other party. Because of this, Japanese businessmen greeting each other are, in reality, engaged in a contest of respect for each other's position in every aspect of living. Traditionally the Japanese lady is subordinate to the Japanese man. This being the case, the Japanese lady always bows lower than the man in the bowing ritual.

It is best that visitors to Japan do not become involved in the bowing ritual. In many such instances the Japanese have a tendency to feel that a mockery is being made of their traditional customs and it is not always appreciated. It is best to simply nod your head in acknowledgment of their presence with an added dash of warmth and a friendly smile *without* the offer to shake hands. Body contact of any kind is not a natural part of Japanese salutations.

At home, we are familiar with the greeter's greeter. He shakes hands with the actions of a lumberjack. He playfully punches his friends in the arm, slaps their backs and usually ends with a warm hug of friendship. His first few meetings with the Japanese are disasters, for in Japan, body contact is a no-no. In contradiction to this statement, it is not uncommon to see two male Japanese walk hand in hand along the side-walks in the major cities throughout Japan.

In the societies of most other countries, the exercise of spoken greetings are complicated by the many titles attached to individuals as a result of their sex, education, religion, marital status, etc. It becomes almost a situation of name, rank and serial number. The fem libbers of today's world have now given us a new title to play with, it is *Ms*. It simply means that it is no one's business whether or not the lady is married.

The Japanese are known for their ritualistic dialogues and manners, which play an important part in their daily lives. They, however, have simplified the spoken greeting as it pertains to titles, to one simple word, *san*. Pronunciation is phonetic *sahn* with a soft *A* sound. This word, san, is added to the end of either the family name or the given name of any Japanese regardless of their sex, marital status, education, politics and encompasses all who are Japanese.

Kenji Tanaka could well be the name of a Japanese man. To correctly speak to him, he could be called either Tanaka-san or Kenji-san. He might be a doctor, or a dentist, a lawyer, an educator with a Ph.D. degree—the use of san is still polite and correct. Kazuko Yamamoto is a young lady who is properly addressed as either Yamamoto-san or Kazuko-san. It is important that visitors to Japan learn this custom and use it liberally with all the Japanese with whom they make an

acquaintance. Whether one uses the family name or the given name depends to a degree on how well you are acquainted.

Among very close friends in Japanese society, san is not always used. A visitor should, however, never presume to drop the use of san without first receiving an indication from the Japanese individual that this would be proper.

The giving of gifts is traditionally a part of Japanese greetings and visitors to Japan making more than casual friendships, such as a business meeting, should prepare themselves to reciprocate in a similar manner. Gifts given under these circumstances should be gift wrapped and are seldom opened at the time of greeting.

Business cards are seemingly as important to the Japanese greeting as is the bowing and the giving of gifts. No self-respecting Japanese businessman or woman would be without a supply of business cards. Visitors to Japan should likewise supply themselves with business cards. If a visitor to Japan would really like a gold star on his or her report card they will have a Japanese translation printed on the back of the business card.

People-watching in Japan is a fantastic experience, as it is throughout the world. The tradition and practice of the Japanese greeting is an art form in itself. In crowded hotel lobbies and on busy sidewalks it sometimes is even disruptive as the maneuvers do take room and a careless visitor might find himself in the midst of a greeting ritual that was not yet ready to be terminated.

Shyness seems to be a Japanese trait that is cultivated and respected. Their greetings are quiet, respectful, and important to those involved. Warmth glows in their eyes but outwardly they display a quiet respect for each other with softly spoken words so as not to disturb anyone else in the area. Jovial laughter and shrieks of delight are reserved for more private surroundings.

5

To Tip or Not To Tip

The matter of tipping, or more politely referred to as the giving of gratuities, is a custom of relatively unknown origin. Most travelers journey in bewilderment throughout the world wondering what is expected of them in this regard. We might as well admit that the custom of tipping is resented by many, reluctantly participated in by others, flagrantly abused by so-called *big shots* who like to throw their weight around and occasionally done intelligently by those people with class who have educated themselves to the variations of this universal custom dependent upon the time and the place and the proper methods to use.

Japan, as every other country in the world, has its own customs. In many ways they are unique in the Land of the Rising Sun, where it is best to know when *to tip* or *not to tip*.

Most guide books and official Japanese government tourist publications tend to describe Japan as a land in which tipping is not a custom. In many ways it is not, especially as related to what is customary in the United States. A very startling example of such a difference is the attitude of the Japanese taxi driver who does not expect to be tipped and in many instances when a tip is offered, the tourist will find the Japanese taxi driver actually refusing to accept the gratuity.

Consider the male American tourist, out of his normal element and needing a haircut. Upon visiting the barber shop in his Tokyo hotel, he finds himself pampered beyond belief. Accustomed to tipping the hair stylist at home, he offers a gratuity which is gracefully refused by the Japanese barber. After much American insistence and Japanese shy refusals, the barber finally accepts the gratuity with a bow of appreciation garnished with an indication of a little embarrassment that he, the Japanese barber, has given in to the client's wishes.

In Western style hotels throughout Japan it is not customary to tip any of the employees. A 10 percent service charge is added to the bill of the guest to cover this expenditure. In reality, however, it is a nice gesture to tip modestly for services rendered by the bellboys, room service waiters, and room maids. Such gratuities should be token gratuities and not of any consequential amounts.

It is also not customary in restaurants throughout Japan to tip your waiter or waitress. It is generally the policy of the majority of restaurants to add a 10 percent service charge to the bill of the customer. It is, however, suggested that a token gratuity be left discreetly under a dish on the table especially in instances where extra service has been given by the waiter or waitress.

Understanding the tipping customs of Japan is a matter of understanding the attitude of the Japanese in service-type employment. Good service is considered a way of life in Japan, even to the degree that many shopkeepers will insist on offering you refreshments or beverages in their shops, whether or not you actually make a purchase. Japanese accepting service-type employment are salaried personnel and they consider it their responsibility to their employer and to the customer to give good service without expecting additional monetary rewards.

Things are just a bit different at a Japanese style hotel, known in Japan as *ryokans*. A ryokan (*rye-oh-kahn*) is a Japanese inn and in many instances is an enlarged version of a Japanese home. Visiting and being an overnight guest in a

ryokan is a delight that should not be missed by any visitor to Japan. The service performed by the staff of a ryokan is beyond belief and the tranquility of the place, the peacefulness of the atmosphere and its exotic simplicity, is relaxation at its utmost. In ryokans, however, it is customary to leave your room maid a gratuity somewhat generous in nature. She is, in reality, your personal servant and remains on duty during your entire stay, catching catnaps in between her responsibilities of keeping your room in order, preparing your bed for a good night's sleep, serving your meals in your room, constantly bringing you hot tea with sweets to tempt your palate, and preparing for your baths in large wooden tubs so you can languish to your heart's delight.

Contrary to the Western custom of offering gratuities openly with cash handed directly to the person involved, the Japanese tip with a gentility and discreetness in harmony with their respect of each other always considering unselfishly the feelings of the other person to be the most important factor. Thus tips offered in Japanese style are always placed in an envelope and, in true Japanese custom, the cash is never visible.

Tourists to Japan will, however, become associated with those Japanese that make their living as guides and tourist car drivers. These persons do expect to be tipped, but will give no indication of such expectations. It has become something of a universal custom to tip tourist guides and drivers according to the quality of the service given. This tip is typically rather generous. In Japan, however, one should do this discreetly using the envelope method and attempt to offer the gratuity without being obvious.

6

Topsy-Turvy Land

Even before you have been in Japan for very long you will notice that the Japanese do things in absolute contrast to what is customary at home. This all will become more and more evident as your journey through *Topsy-Turvy Land,* as it is sometimes called, continues.

Aside from the obvious fact that all traffic in Japan moves in the right-hand style and all the drivers sit on the right side of the vehicle, the American tourist suddenly became aware of the topsy-turvy atmosphere when he waved goodbye to a pretty Japanese girl he had been talking with in front of his Tokyo hotel. He waved in the typical American manner. The girl responded by turning around and walking back towards him. He had discovered that such a gesture in Japan means *come here.*

The same tourist was startled to observe Japanese carpenters at work on a building near his hotel when he noticed that in sawing lumber they draw the saw toward their body instead of pushing against the lumber. He also noticed that the same was true when they planed or shaved the work with a hand plane.

"That's a little dangerous," he thought to himself.

Upon returning to the lobby of his hotel he noticed that the Japanese reading books and magazines started at, to him, the back cover of the book or magazine. He began to think that he should be walking on the ceiling instead of the floor. He had already learned that the Japanese don't shake hands but prefer to bow to each other instead.

"This is really going to be interesting," he admitted to himself.

The Japanese many times do things in a very different way and much is not only tradition, but is due to the historic fact that the country and its people were isolated for so long from any outside influence and simply developed their own way of life. This has not changed for generations and even in a modern westernized city, such as Tokyo, these differences can be observed readily and frequently.

There are many interesting and fascinating differences encompassing all aspects of life. Good beef cattle don't graze but are massaged daily and fed a diet of beer with other feed. Horses are backed into their stalls. A wife always walks behind her husband. The Japanese will not usually sleep facing north because this is the position in which the dead are placed.

A Japanese family moving into a new neighborhood will call on their neighbors first rather than the other way around. It's sort of a *Welcome Wagon* in reverse. A set of dishes in Japan comes in combinations of 5 or 10 instead of 6 or 12. Doors don't usually open in and out but slide in grooves. Revolving doors are a puzzle to the Japanese because the doors don't seem to move in the correct cycle of rotation, such doors being part of modern architecture and the Westernization of Japan.

If you should hear a Japanese sucking air into his mouth, it is an indication of respect. It is not customary to give names to streets in Japan and the numbers of the buildings in a given block are assigned according to the date of construction and have little or no relation to the building next door. A Japanese stirs his tea counterclockwise instead of clockwise. They don't say *northeast*, but instead prefer *eastnorth*, etc. A typical Japanese motto translated to English might be, "Don't do unto to others as you wouldn't have them do unto you."

Throughout much of the world it has been a long standing custom to refer to a ship in the person of *she*. One legend of the sea states that this reference is based on the fact that a ship is a beautiful thing upon which to feast the eye. Her lines are smooth and she moves through the water with gracefulness personified by regally gowned ladies gliding across the marbled floors of royal courts throughout the world, her masters seeking to control her ways and whims. In Japan, however, a ship is referred to as *he*.

Our ever-observant tourist contemplates all this *upsidedownishness* as his wife tries on a kimono with a floppy hat on her head, the two Japanese salesladies giggling quietly to themselves. Not only is it considered bad taste to wear a hat of any kind when dressed in a kimono, she had innocently wrapped the garment in typical Western fashion, right over left. This is correct in Japan only when the lady is dead, otherwise it is left over right.

7

Men First, Please

The man comes first in Japan. That's their tradition. Not that the Japanese women totally agree with this situation, but they do seem rather resigned to its continued practice.

As in almost every other area of the world, the Japanese woman is beginning to assert herself for more recognition in business, society, and all other phases of life. It is still very common, however, to give preference to the male members of the Japanese populace.

For centuries it has been traditional in Japan that the wife carry the packages on a shopping spree. For centuries the Japanese woman has traditionally walked behind her husband in public as if following him. To a Westerner such tradition seems subservient, but to most Japanese women over the years, it has been part of their natural life to relate to their men in such a fashion. Most Japanese girls have been raised to consider the man the most important factor in the human relationship and it is her natural instinct to treat him with the utmost care and respect.

Many visiting women of other nationalities have been and are being shocked as they find themselves being pushed aside by Japanese men entering buildings, mounting an escalator, entering or leaving an elevator. It simply isn't their custom or way of life to yield to the woman in such situations and it never enters their heads to do so in most cases. It is not rudeness, to them it is absolutely normal.

The human congestion of Japan, and particularly its major cities, has caused the Japanese to be seemingly rude and ruthless in crowds. There seems to be no limits to the capacity of an elevator, a stairway, a doorway, a car on a commuter train, a bus, a streetcar or any other kind of people-containing unit. The operators of the commuter trains in the major cities, at key stations, actually employ people whose job it is to push people into the trains well beyond reasonable capacity. It is not uncommon to find yourself swept up in a mass of humanity that promptly places you on a train that isn't going where you want to go, or to find yourself suddenly on the outside of a train that you wanted to stay on until the next station. It is just part of the morning and evening rush.

Elevators in Japanese office buildings are amazing pieces of apparatus that seem to have rubber walls that expand to limitless capacity as proven in a story related by an American couple visiting Tokyo.

They had visited a pearl gallery in downtown Tokyo and were waiting for an elevator to arrive. When one finally did, there was just room enough for the two of them to get in and turn around as the door closed. Already overburdened with a heavy human load the elevator stopped at the very next floor and the doors opened. Much to our friends' surprise, they were confronted with a well-dressed Japanese businessman, briefcase in hand, running toward the open door to force himself into the elevator. The husband, being rather rubbery about the waist, stood firm and the Japanese gentleman bounced back into the hall and the elevator proceeded downward with its laughing load of sardines.

All of this is in strange contrast to the natural gentility of the Japanese. It is in contrast to their natural shyness. It is in contrast to their respect for each other in their social lives and their inherent respect of patience, understanding, and tranquility brought out in their religious philosophies. It is in contrast to the importance of sociability in their business

world. It can only be blamed on the congestion of their land and the crowded conditions of their cities.

If such conditions become irritating to the visitor, he should merely join the throng and make a game of it all. There is a great deal of truth in the old adage, "When in Rome, do as the Romans do."

8

Kamikaze!

The usually robust American feebly walked into the lobby of his hotel in Tokyo feeling as though his knees were about to give out. His wife was not far away, but she was standing just inside the revolving door trembling from head to foot and looking like a ghost—her face a portrait of horror and fright.

Numbly they recovered their composure and eventually made it to the elevator and the safety of their room where in private they slowly recovered from their first taxicab ride in Tokyo.

Ordering a bucket of ice from room service, they break out a bottle of scotch to calm their nerves. The Japanese room service waiter who arrives with the bucket of ice is not surprised at the ashen faces and shaken humans he sees. The waiter places the bucket of ice on a nearby table, politely bows, and says to them, "Ah so, you have first *kamikaze* taxi ride in Tokyo, so solly," as he bows politely and backs out of the room.

Traffic in Tokyo is unbelievable, what with 12 million people in residence there, this fact is not surprising. The taxi cabs are even more unbelievable and the men who drive them must have nerves of steel.

The natural reflexes of American visitors is out of whack in the first place as traffic in Japan operates British style with the right-hand drive. Even stepping off a curb is dangerous as the traffic is coming from the opposite direction than your instinct tells you. Even walking in crowds one soon learns that the pedestrians move in the same fashion and an American often feels as though he is walking upstream in a rushing tide of humanity.

Tokyo is well-known for its high rate of traffic fatalities but in strange contrast it is extremely rare to ever see a vehicle that is not in perfect condition. Even the crazy taxicabs don't have dents and they all look as though they are brand new. Their drivers are clean, the taxicabs are clean, the drivers often wear a neat uniform cap and are quite commonly wearing a pair of white gloves that appear to have just come from the laundry. A feather duster is part of the standard taxicab equipment and is always in evidence on the shelf of the rear window. The duster is used daily, several times, to keep the cab clean and shining brightly—to be ready for its next journey of terror in Tokyo.

Getting a taxicab at your Tokyo hotel is not usually a difficult thing, though sometimes it does mean standing in an orderly line and taking your turn. Most Japanese taxi drivers have little or no use of the English language and it is always necessary to carry with you a Japanese translation of your destination. To attempt to flag down a cruising taxicab in Tokyo is quite another matter and it is usually necessary to go to a nearby train station, department store, or hotel and wait in an orderly line for your turn to come. Many Japanese taxi drivers hesitate to pick up Westerners that flag them on the street, mostly because they are afraid of the language problem.

Our shaken friends, now safe in their hotel room, had been in the Ginza district of downtown Tokyo on the day of their first taxi experience. After spending the morning on a sightseeing trip, they had ended their tour downtown in order to do some shopping. They were carrying Japanese cards that identified their hotel and after many unsuccessful attempts at flagging a taxicab on the street they found a taxi line near one of the large department stores. The line moved quite rapidly

and soon it came their turn to get a taxi. As the husband approached the taxi and reached for the back door, the door suddenly burst open and he landed in a heap of packages in the street causing his wife to scream with alarm.

Most Japanese taxicabs, not just those in Tokyo, have automatic rear doors which are opened and closed by the driver. Not being aware of this, the tourist had been felled in innocent bewilderment. Most taxi drivers in Japan do not like you to open or close these rear doors manually as it is hard on the mechanism. Needless to say the experience had been hard on our friends. Now suddenly outright fear overtook their embarrassment and bruises as the taxi suddenly surged into traffic and went roaring through Tokyo as though out of control. The driver passed everyone else on what appeared to be the wrong side in a now and then game of chicken on a narrow street, narrowly missing the opponent, and making left and right turns to the seemingly wrong side of the street. Unable to speak to the driver who never stopped long enough for them to escape, they rode in horror during what they were sure was to be their last moments on earth.

All taxicabs in the major Japanese cities have meters and they are relatively inexpensive. There is no need to pay anymore than the amount of yen shown on the meter as Japanese taxi drivers do not expect to be tipped. Some frequent visitors to Tokyo, have taken to tipping taxi drivers out of gratefulness for a safe journey. Strangely enough, to the visitors at least, some of the drivers still refuse to accept tips.

The right-hand drive situation is frightening at best until one gets used to the motions and the expectations. I recall one woman that had a frightening experience which brought screams of laughter to her fellow travelers.

Enroute from Tokyo to Kamakura our sightseeing bus had made a stop in Yokohama to visit the silk museum. The woman had become intrigued with a shop across the street from the bus and had gone to the shop to look around. She soon noticed that the bus was full and ready to leave and in her rush to cross the street she was almost struck by a car. She was frightened and her face was white as she boarded the bus.

"Did you see what happened out there?" her quavering voice asked.

"Sure I did. So what?" I said, trying to pass the incident off.

"Well, how would you feel if you had almost been hit by a black Toyota being driven by a large white dog?" she answered.

It seemed to her, of course, that the big white dog was sitting where the driver should have been.

9

Take 'em Off, Take 'em Off

"Take it off, take it off, cried the boys in the rear." It seems that I heard this cry the last time I was in a burlesque theater in the U.S.A., at which time I was also shocked to find my mathematics teacher sitting in the front row.

Many's the time a tourist has been heard walking around mumbling, half to himself, this famous old American burlesque expression. After a few days it seems that you spend more time out of your shoes than in them moving about Japan.

Many visitors assume that the Japanese custom of removing your shoes is connected with religious life. They become aware that it is a custom to remove one's shoes upon entering all Japanese homes, medical offices, restaurants (Japanese style), as well as shrines and temples as a general rule. This is particularly true when entering all rooms or areas that are covered with tatami mats. Tatami mats being those thick and luxurious Japanese grass squares with the exotic smell and subtle softness so restful to weary feet and tired legs.

Generally it is the policy of most homes, restaurants, and other places to provide paper slippers to wear in place of your outdoor shoes. It is equally common and well-accepted to walk in stocking feet or even barefooted—some travelers face their first problem in Japan upon discovering a hole in a sock! However, slippers with hard soles are not acceptable and it is best to come equipped with woolen slip-ons or other slippers of soft material for protection and warmth when needed.

A visit to Nikko, usually an all-day affair from Tokyo, is one of the world's most famous sightseeing adventures and it is there, but more specifically at the Toshogu shrine in Nikko, that a daily performance of human comedy occurs that would delight the court jesters of old.

Nikko is as popular, if not more so, with Japanese tourists than it is with visitors from other lands. Since it is required that everyone must remove their shoes before entering the Toshogu shrine, a natural stage has developed over the years in a wooded theater. On this stage, 365 days of the year, just outside the entrance to the Toshogu shrine, there is a comedy to end all comedies. By theatrical standards it is a large production for it takes two complete casts of characters, the Japanese tourists and the visitors from the Western world. Each cast of characters has their own stage door directly adjacent to each other and the performance goes something like this.

A group of American tourists arrives and is instructed on the procedure to follow for the removal of their shoes.

A large group of Japanese tourists comes shuffling across the stones, led by a guide carrying what appears to be a battle flag. No self-respecting group of Japanese tourists would travel without a flag-bearing leader. There must be at least 75 people in this particular group and they rapidly and deftly slip out of their shoes, as if in perpetual motion, leaving their shoes scattered about their entrance and padding softly into the shrine to enjoy the delights inside.

Meanwhile back at the American entrance, members of our group are seated all over the place, legs askew, garters and girdles in view, helping each other up and down, finding a locker in which to place their shoes for safekeeping. Safekeeping from whom? Who wants old shoes?

From within the din of the mumbling and grumbling of the American group we hear, "Flo, I wish you'd told me to wear my loafers, I can't get these damn laces untied."

"Quit complaining, Max. How do you think I feel with this big run I just got in my hose," Flo retorts. "Max! there's no more empty lockers, what are we going to do with our shoes? They'll get stolen."

"You go see the shrine; I'll watch the shoes."

"Oh no, you don't, I'm not going in there alone."

Of course, during this performance the large Japanese group has returned from touring the shrine and have deftly slipped back into their shoes and have vanished toward other vistas of beauty led by their fearless flag-bearer.

Such performances of comparative innocent cloddishness and studied gracefulness go on daily throughout Japan, for that matter throughout much of the Eastern world. It's just a simple matter of customs and it's quite obvious which of the cast of characters is out of their element.

No visitor to Japan should ever fear thievery. The Japanese, as a whole, have too much self-pride and self-respect to steal anything—especially used shoes!

10

Dancing in the Night

After their previous day's tour to Nikko, Max and Flo enjoyed a leisurely day free of any plan in Tokyo and as the sun set slowly behind Tokyo Tower it suddenly occurred to Florence that she would like to experience some of Tokyo's nightlife.

"Might even get Max to do a little dancing," she thought.

Meanwhile, Max had his own thought about Tokyo nightlife and was wondering how he could get away from Flo and visit some of the exotic spots he had heard about and had seen ads for in the English-language newspapers. He had become aware that bar hostesses were quite the thing in Japan and his natural male curiosity was nagging at his brain and ego.

"Max" said Flo, "let's go nightclubbing tonight. I'd sort of like to see the bright lights and maybe we can find a place to dance."

At this point Max knew full well that his secret plans were out the window so he agreed to take Flo out on the town. Max attempted to get the tour director on the telephone to ask his advice about where to go, but he was enjoying a rest from his duties and couldn't be found.

The hotel where Max and Flo were staying was located in the Akasaka district of Tokyo, an area well-known for its abundance of plushy night clubs, bright lights, and little narrow streets abounding with small bars, geisha houses, and mysterious looking stairways to who knows where.

Soon Max and Flo found themselves seated in a booth in a large and very plush Western style nightclub. It was not yet showtime and Max leaned back in the booth pondering the fact that it had cost a few thousand Japanese yen just to get into the club. His mental calculations into dollars wasn't functioning too well, so he shrugged it off and tried to look forward to the show, a few drinks, some good music, and maybe a peek or two at some Japanese girls.

"Might even give in and dance with Flo," he thought to himself.

It wasn't long before someone took their order and they soon found their drinks on the table in front of them. It also wasn't long before two very pretty Japanese girls came and sat in the booth with Max and Flo and proceeded to get into a conversation with them in English. Feeling it was the proper thing to do, Max ordered drinks for the girls feeling, at the same time, that it was rather strange these girls so willingly joined them as if it was the most natural thing to do. Shortly after the drinks came for the girls, various dishes of peanuts, potato chips, candy, popcorn and other goodies appeared on the table in front of them.

Max and Flo did get in a dance or two between conversations with the Japanese girls. After about two hours of this, during which there had been a rather standard nightclub show (none of which they understood because it was in Japanese), Max decided it was time to leave and try another place. He asked for his bill whereupon the girls promptly left the table with a polite good-bye.

It really was too bad that Max had not been able to obtain advice from the tour director earlier because if he had he would have been better prepared for the presentation of his bill which on first sight appeared to be a settlement of the Japanese national debt. These Japanese nightclubs should really have oxygen or at least smelling salts available for unsuspecting tourists at the time they present them with their tab.

Including the two girls, Max had ordered about five drinks apiece. The price for each was astronomically high. There was a charge for each dish of goodies that had been brought to their table. There was an hourly charge for each girl's presence and to add to this whole transaction, a 10 percent surcharge for service on the entire amount and another 10 percent tax on the accumulated total—Max was bankrupt!

Fortunately, the Japanese nightclub owners don't rely on the tourists to fill their clubs and to be their prime source of income. Rather they rely on the Japanese businessmen themselves who use these clubs to entertain their clients at the expense of their employers. The exception to these are the nightclubs found in the major hotels. Since much of their business comes from tourists they are similar in operation to those of the West.

Large Japanese cities are a blaze of lights at night and the nightlife is plentiful, but expensive. After an experience such as that of Max and Flo most tourists do not go nightclubbing in Japan again. At about midnight it seems that the cities close down and they roll up the sidewalks. Apparently the Japanese wife insists that her husband be home by midnight because they all hurry off about that time as if in fear of becoming pumpkins.

11

Ōki Onaka!

Our example of the American tourist, Max, is the proud possessor of an *ōki onaka!* He, however, does not yet know what that is and the curiousity that it is going to create particularly with the Japanese children. Max's ōki onaka is part and parcel of his being and his very personality. He carries it with him wherever he goes and some suspect he does so with pride while others suspect he does so with some discomfort. On the surface it appears that Max is very proud of his ōki onaka; it is a rather large ōki onaka so possibly he should be proud. He has often been observed patting his ōki onaka; he has often been observed filling it with great pleasure. His ōki onaka is a tremendous support for his camera as well as his trousers. After all it is not everyone who has as well formed an ōki onaka, as does Max.

Even though physical contact between people is considered a no-no under most circumstances in Japan, many Japanese have patted Max's ōki onaka and smiled with obvious pleasure in return. Ōki onaka in Japanese is *big stomach*. Ōki onaka is a part and parcel of every Buddha in Japan. Since it is considered good luck to rub the ōki onaka of Buddha it is

likewise considered a compliment to Max to be in possession of such a nice ōki onaka and they cannot resist touching it for good luck.

During his first few days in Japan, Max has thoroughly enjoyed the attention he has received regarding his abdominal protuberance. At home everyone usually looks with some disdain at this part of him and he is endlessly being teased by his friends about his big stomach. All of a sudden it is something to be proud of and he is living in complete enjoyment of his new found adoration.

Flo on the other hand is completely disgusted with the entire matter and shrugs in embarrassment as pretty girls, children, and other Japanese make such a fun issue of her husband's appearance.

Most visitors to Japan have the opportunity to visit the city of Kamakura not far from Tokyo. In Kamakura sits a bronze image of Buddha more than 700 years old. It is considered to be the largest image of Buddha sitting outside in the open air; it had once been housed in a large building which was destroyed long ago by a tidal wave. This particular Buddha is very popular with Japanese tourists as well as foreigners and the grounds are always crowded with a mixture of humanity.

Buddha's large stomach represents a well-fed human being in obvious happy contentment with his lot in life. Patience, tranquility and contentment being important ingredients in the lives of Japanese, this image is important but is not worshipped in the same sense that idols, images and icons are worshipped in other parts of the world.

Max got a great deal of pleasure out of seeing this Buddha, especially when there were so many people making obvious comparisons between the Buddha and himself. During the visit to the Buddha of Kamakura, Max had observed that Japanese were leaving gifts of flowers, food and sake as offerings to the Buddha. He found this most interesting. In fact, he found it so interesting that he was observed leaving one of his favorite cigars on the altar as he left.

While many of the Japanese were spreading the smoke from incense altars on afflicted portions of their bodies as a blessing for a cure to their ills, Max walked proudly past the incense burners without batting an eyelash and it seemed that his waist line had grown just a bit bigger.

12

Rub-a-Dub-Dub

Having left the Buddha of Kamakura behind and after joining with their American tourist friends at a Japanese restaurant where they were served a Chinese lunch, Max and Flo are seated side by side on their chartered bus, Max enjoying his usual cigar while the rest of the group mumbles about it appropriately. As they pass through Odawara, Max slips into peaceful sleep with sweet memories of the Buddha. His cigar slips from his fingers into the aisle of the bus and six shoes simultaneously stomp the cigar into oblivion.

As Max sleeps peacefully on, the bus begins its steady climb into the Hakone National Park. Its destination is the Fujiya Hotel in the village of Miyanoshita. Soon the tour director takes the microphone to talk about the Fujiya Hotel and tell some of its history as well as explain to the group what is included in their visit to the Fujiya Hotel.

"Ladies and gentlemen, I am delighted to tell you that your stay at the Fujiya Hotel includes a massage..."

At the sound of the word massage, Max sits bolt upright in his seat, "What'd he say, Flo?"

"He said you get a massage at the Fujiya Hotel included in the cost of the tour, stupid," Flo answered.

All of a sudden Max's brain recalls all those stories he had heard for years about the great Japanese massage girls and how they walk on your back and all that sort of stuff. Maybe even a little extra service, he thought, silently to himself.

For a Japanese masseuse to walk on Max's back, considering his well formed ōki onaka, would be something similar to walking on a teeter-totter, if someone were to even consider it.

Most visitors to Japan have much to learn about the customs of bathing, steaming and massaging Japanese style. If the Japanese have a fetish, it is cleanliness. The bath is a joy to behold and it is an integral part of daily life of a Japanese family. At vacation time many Japanese visit their favorite hot spring resorts to enjoy the natural mineral baths, steam baths and the massages so adeptly administered by masseuses and masseurs. Such is the case at the Fujiya in Miyanoshita.

Tour guides have been this route many times and should always explain to groups some of the facts regarding *the bath* in Japan and the related pleasures of the senses.

First and most important, it must be learned that the Japanese *never* contaminate a bath tub with soap. All Japanese bathing areas or bathrooms are equipped with small pans or pails which they dip into the tub to pour water over their bodies. It is then that the Japanese soap themselves. (It is interesting to note that a good Japanese wife always does this for her husband.) This is followed with a rinsing of themselves after which they immerse themselves in their deep tubs up to their necks and soak in the ultra hot water. (It is interesting, again, to note that many Japanese couples soak together.) Since all of this usually occurs as the husband gets home from work, after which food is taken and sake is shared, it all becomes somewhat exotic and the fetish for the bath is understood.

While many a lurid story has been told about the typical Japanese massage parlor, it is generally just that—a massage parlor and nothing else. It is usually equipped with a steam cabinet and after steaming the customer is bathed in traditional Japanese fashion (the customer is, of course, naked)

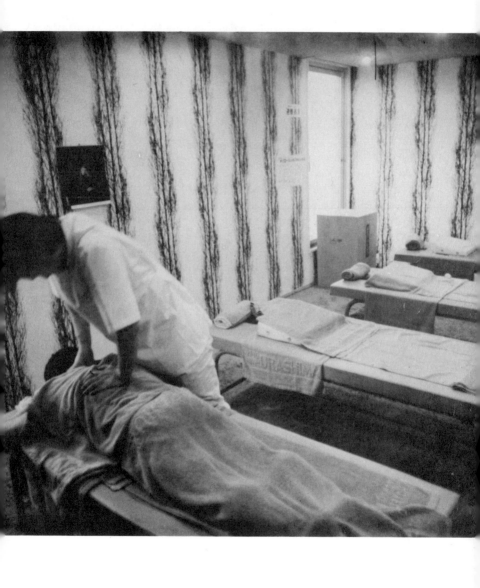

then massaged. A regular Japanese massage is vigorous to the point of being anything but sexy. Some masseuses and masseurs do walk on the backs of the customers, but do so very lightly with the tips of their toes only along the spinal column while they support their weight against an adjacent wall and not onto the back of the customer. It is really a form of spinal manipulation designed to calm the nerves and relax the customer.

Many visitors to Japan have the impression that the Japanese bathe in public bath houses which are coeducational and men, women and children all do it together. This may still be true in some remote areas of the country, however, the public bath houses of Japan are now segregated by sex. Soaping is always done outside the main pool and the pool is used only for soaking. It is, however, becoming more and more the custom to have a private bath in their own homes.

Test the water before you enter. The Japanese, you see, have become accustomed to extremely hot water which is scalding to many visitors. I also recommend the family baths to couples as an exotic adventure not soon to be forgotten. They have been credited with strengthening many marriages of couples on tour. The hotels will often supply *yukatas,* which are light kimonos, for use as bathrobes and not to be taken as souvenirs.

13

Sw-o-o-o-o-sh

Max and Flo are about to be sw-o-o-o-shed. They've never been swooshed before and are not quite sure just exactly what is in store for them. Their tour director has been swooshed many times, but for the fun of the game he chooses not to give away his secrets about swooshing. His smugness about the whole matter is very upsetting to Max.

In his frustration Max turns to Flo and says: "I wonder what our martinet tour leader is up to today?"

"Don't get so upset. A little swooshing is good for the soul, now and then," Flo answers.

"But he looks like a cat that just swallowed a canary," says Max.

"Maybe he did, but I'm not going looking for the feathers and neither are you, Max. For once let's just be cool about the situation," says Flo.

Our group of touring Americans is riding in a bus down the mountainside from Hakone National Park enroute to the Pacific seacoast town of Atami where they will board a train to take them to Osaka. What they are really heading for is a ride on the world's fastest train—the Bullet Train. Known officially

in Japan as *Shinkansen,* which literally means New Trunk Line.

In ancient Japan the route traveled between Kyoto and Tokyo was known as the Tokaido Road. It naturally followed that the first railroad built between these two cities was called the Tokaido Line. In 1964, the same year that Japan hosted the Olympic Games, the Bullet Train route was completed and originally called the New Tokaido Line. Bullet Train was a name given to the train itself based on its appearance which is ballistic in form. As it streaks across the countryside, its distinctive blue and white paint job leaving an optical streak of color, it appears to be a swooshing mechanical monster of unbelievable proportions.

Upon arrival at the Atami Bullet Train station, the tour director gathers his group together and enters the modern station. After gaining clearance for his reserved seat tickets he takes the group via two flights of escalators to the main station platform and stations them precisely along a painted line indicating an entrance to car #14. He has done this early, mostly for his own enjoyment.

There are two types of Bullet Trains known as *Hikari* and *Kodama.* Hikari is the super express that does not stop at Atami, instead it travels through the station at incredible speed presenting a sight and an experience not soon forgotten. Suddenly an alarm is sounded, one of the Hikari trains is about to burst out of a tunnel nearby and roar through the Atami station within a few feet of where the group is standing. He says nothing to them about this and instead contents himself with watching the expressions on their faces as the train swooshes past in seconds.

Soon their train, a Kodama, arrives and mayhem occurs as the group scrambles aboard during the train's 60-second stop. Inside they find a brightly lighted coach of fantastic dimensions and airline style seating. They barely get seated before they roar off into another tunnel soon to be flying over the mile-long welded rails at a maximum speed of 131 miles per hour. Inside, however, it is incredibly smooth and there is little sensation of speed. Our friends have been swooshed and they have enjoyed every minute of it. At the same time they

have suddenly become dramatically aware of the ability of the Japanese to engineer and operate such a rail system. The Bullet Train is undoubtedly the world's most efficient and safely operated railroad.

The engineering accomplishment of the Bullet Train is outstanding in the field of mass transportation. It covers the distance of 313 miles between Tokyo and Osaka in about 3 hours and 10 minutes on the Hikari trains. It is a two-track, wide-gauge system with an overhead electrical power supply. The entire system is electronically computer controlled from a central headquarters in Tokyo. It seems to be accident proof as indicated by its flawless safety record. Between the hours of 6:00 a.m. and 8:30 p.m., daily trains leave the Tokyo and Osaka stations at about 10 minute intervals and interweave themselves along the system combining the super express, Hikari, and the limited express, Kodama.

Both types of the trains which operate at high speeds are automatically controlled by the master unit in Tokyo. The system has measuring devices so sensitive that high winds, heavy rainfall or earthquakes above a certain density will either slow the train or completely turn off the system automatically stopping all enroute operations.

Extension of this system has now been accomplished beyond Osaka to the city of Okayama, a distance of about 100 miles. By 1975, it is estimated that such a rail line will be in operation to the city of Fukuoka on the island of Kyushu in southern Japan. Additional extensions are planned to the north of Tokyo ultimately to include service to the island of Hokkaido via an undersea tunnel connecting the islands of Honshu and Hokkaido.

The Japanese are proud of their accomplishment in the field of mass transportation even though the average Japanese now takes the Bullet Train for granted. This pride is justly deserved.

14

We Know Where You're Going

A better title to this chapter might have been "Proper Potty Positions." This important aspect of daily life is very different in Japan and, in many ways, is hilarious in its potential humor.

While aboard the Bullet Train between Atami and Osaka, Max and Flo had both noticed that the train was equipped with two types of restrooms. The doors were labeled in English and Japanese indicating whether they were Western style toilets or Japanese style toilets.

Max left his seat and went to the you-know-where and selected the one labeled Western style toilet. He was immediately surprised to notice that directly above the toilet seat was a sign in Japanese with stick drawings of human beings obviously giving instructions as to the proper usage of this sanitary facility. Max began to laugh so hard that he almost forgot why he was there.

These signs are placed in the Western style toilets on the train for a very real reason. Many country Japanese have not had the opportunity to use or experience a Western style toilet before and its apparatus is as strange to them as the Japanese style toilet is to the Westerner.

This situation also reminded Max of a day previous in Tokyo when he had gone to the men's room at his hotel and, upon entry, had found a female attendant cleaning the rest room. He had stalled, fumbled, washed his face three times, washed his hands four times, blew his nose twice, combed what hair he had until his scalp was sore and still she didn't leave. Max finally left and went to his room. He soon learned that it is customary for women to be the restroom attendants and that they couldn't care less what you are there for and just simply expect you to accomplish your purpose and leave. Many a male visitor to Japan for the first time has almost permanently injured himself when suddenly confronted by the entrance of a female attendant into the men's room.

The Japanese style toilet is indeed a strange piece of apparatus to Westerners. It merely consists of a ceramic or tile slot in the floor with a drain at one end. It is almost flush with the level of the floor and one wonders exactly how you approach this device depending on gender of the user. In many country areas the toilets are coeducational and the device in the floor is large enough to accommodate several people at the same time. Such was the case after the tourists had crossed the Inland Sea and arrived at the city of Beppu on the island of Kyushu.

While in the Beppu area the tour group went sightseeing. About half way through the all-day tour, the tour guide had made a stop for a *telephone call* as she referred to it. This, of course, meant a rest stop. There had been a large toilet building with two entrances and two separate rooms, but since they did not have any markings on them, it had to be considered that these were the coeducational toilets they had heard about. Following Western customs, their group split with the men using one room and the women using the other. Unknown to the women, however, the men could hear them conversing about the strange facility. It was difficult for the men to keep from breaking out in loud laughter because what they heard coming from the other side of the partition went something like this:

"Which is the front of this thing?"

"Do they really sit on this?"

"I wish I had better aim."

"If you could do this in a kimono you could get a job with the circus."

"This pose reminds me of a baseball catcher."

"What do we do if some men come in?"

"Get that lady with the camera out of here."

"I'm gonna need an acupuncture treatment after I get up from this thing."

A word to the wise: when in the countryside of Japan, don't drink the water. It's not that the water is impure, it just makes life simpler!

15

The Diet Beguine

The word *beguine*, according to Webster, comes from the French word *beguin* meaning flirtation. The Japanese diet is certainly a flirtation with food in its strictest interpretation as the pleasures of the eye are as important as the pleasures of the stomach.

For the past few days Max had been observing the Japanese at table with a great deal of interest. While he and Florence had not yet attempted to savor the delights of Japanese traditional food, they had noticed the artistic presentation of Japanese meals and the apparent relish with which the Japanese feasted their eyes upon the colorful array. It seemed to them that the Japanese admired the food almost more than they enjoyed its delicate tastes. Such, in reality, is the case.

One day during a lunch break in their sightseeing activities they decided to sample Japanese food at a little shop in Beppu. They had previously noticed, on many occasions, the neat and colorful displays of meals in the windows of Japanese restaurants. The displays were actually plastic representations of the items on the menu. They were so lifelike that it was difficult to tell them from the genuine article.

After considerable consideration and gesturing, Max and Florence decided on a large bowl of noodles for lunch and they entered the little restaurant with much curiosity. A smiling Japanese hostess met them at the door and took them back outside to show her what they wanted in the display window. They paid in advance and received a ticket for their selection. In short order their noodles arrived accompanied by disposable chopsticks and a large ceramic spoon. The spoon was clumsy and uncomfortable to use, but how does one eat soup with chopsticks? Max was seen studying the end of one of his chopsticks as if hoping it would become a straw. Florence was observed twitching in her seat and looking at her luncheon companions as if wishing that one of them would hand her an instruction sheet in English, of course.

Then Max and Florence noticed the secret. It is more appropriate to say that they heard the secret. Those Japanese who had also ordered noodles for lunch were deftly twirling the noodles around their chopsticks and swiftly swooping them into their mouths, heads bowed close to the giant soup bowls, sucking and slurping the slippery threads with vigorous delight as though Emily Post was a thing of the past. It all kind of made Max and Florence think of a vacuum cleaner repair shop. To enjoy the delicious broth, the Japanese energetically lifted the gigantic soup bowls to their lips as if drinking a mammoth-sized cup of ceremonial tea.

The Japanese diet is one of the world's most unique in its content and its display. Restaurants in Japan are customarily devoted to one dish and a choice of restaurants is generally made, by the Japanese, according to the dish they wish to enjoy. So if one wants noodles, it is to a noodle shop that one goes. If one wants barbecued meat on a skewer, it is to a *yakitori* shop that one ventures. This procedure continues on through the Japanese spectrum of delicate delights that tempt the eye, the ear, and the esophagus.

The Japanese depend to a great extent on the bountiful sea that surrounds their beautiful country as a source of their food. There is little in the sea that the Japanese have not found a use for as food. Raw fish is an important part of their gastronomy and it is presented in two basic forms, *sushi* and *sashimi.*

A Japanese housewife customarily shops everyday for the dietary needs of her family and one of the most important items is the seafood and its most important characteristic is its freshness. Eating raw seafood requires that the meat be almost alive and the Japanese housewife has almost a fetish about its quality as do the chefs of the Japanese restaurants that serve raw fish.

Sushi is often referred to as the sandwich of Japan and sushi shops are used by the Japanese in the same way that Americans use the corner coffee shop. Sushi in its presentation is a delight to the eye. Small pieces of raw fish or delicately seasoned pickles are rolled in an encasement of lightly vinegared rice and then wrapped in tissue paper thin sheets of seaweed, black in color. The pieces are dipped according to taste in sauces seasoned by soy sauce, sweet sake, mustard and other palate pleasing preparations.

Sashimi, on the other hand, is simply thin fillets of raw fish artfully arranged on artistic dishes garnished with a scallion or two and eaten in the same sauce-dipping fashion as sushi. Most westerners who bring themselves to indulge in the delights of sushi and sashimi usually take a liking to this aspect of Japanese dietary enchantment.

In the basement of their hotel in Beppu, Max and Flo had noticed an attractive Japanese restaurant and one evening decided they would try another of the Japanese meals. Little did they understand that they were about to participate in a Japanese eating adventure that tends to be downright horrifying in nature.

Hanging from the ceiling of this particular restaurant was an array of blow fish. Upon questioning their waiter, who spoke a little English, Max learned that these decorations were *fugu fish,* a breed of blow fish found in the Inland Sea near their hotel. He also learned that the fish were deadly poisonous and that there were stories in abundance about Japanese who had died experiencing the pleasures of its flesh. Max, being of sound mind and body, ordered some for himself and Florence

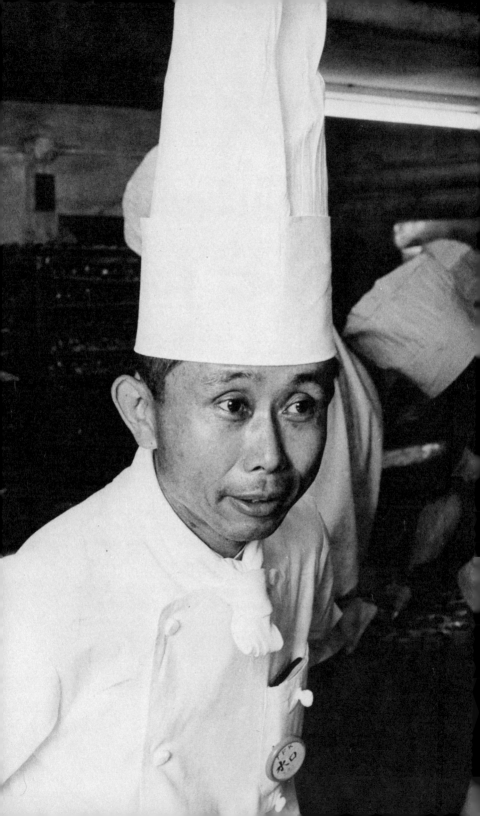

with considerable curiosity (the least of which were the clauses in his life insurance policy).

Upon presentation of their fugu fish meal, Max was entranced by the transparent quality of the meat's thin fillets and silently wondered if that was what was about to become of his own flesh. Chilled to the marrow as he was, he gingerly tasted the meat expecting at any moment to experience spasms of his last moments on earth as its vital signs slowly stopped functioning.

Meanwhile Florence sat trembling and silently thinking that this was all rather ridiculous as her taste buds now experienced an uncontrollable urge for a steak sandwich, medium rare.

In reality, few Japanese, or any members of the human race, for that matter, actually succumb to the deadly fugu fish. The Japanese government has a licensing policy for the butchers of fugu fish that is strictly adhered to and it is seldom that any accidents occur. But it does seem that the Japanese really do enjoy this form of gourmet roulette and participate in the meal with a great deal of chattering and abandon.

What with fish eyes, octopus, eel, squid, sea anemone, sea weed, fugu fish, sea urchins and endless other items of menu curiosities, the Japanese Diet Beguine is truly unique and is a trip in itself.

16

The Wedding Broker

While Max and Flo were having their dinner in the Japanese restaurant they had discovered in the basement of their hotel in Beppu, a large Japanese wedding party arrived and quickly ordered the specialty of the house, fugu fish. It seemed a strange anachronism to Max and Flo that a couple starting their life together would participate in such a potentially fatal feast. It seemed to be a rather rakish spin of the wheel of fortune.

The sight of the wedding party reminded Max and Florence of their recent voyage on the Inland Sea between Osaka and Beppu. There had been many newlyweds on the ship and they had had an interesting conversation with one of the couples who spoke English quite well. When the ship called at Takamatsu there had been many wedding parties on the dock seeing other newlyweds off on their honeymoons. The young Japanese wife that had befriended Max and Flo proceeded to explain many of the customs related to Japanese marriages.

Florence had been intrigued with the distinctive black and white headdress of the Japanese brides as well as with their beautiful kimonos. She had also noticed that many of the Japanese brides were dressed Western style for traveling and she felt that this was a little disconcerting in light of how beautiful the Japanese girls are in their kimonos. Her new-found friend had explained that the female attendants in the seemingly formal black kimonos dotted with a small white pattern, were those that were married. The lady attendants in colorful kimonos were still unwed and their colorful kimonos were intended to catch the eye of the available males.

From outward observance, shyness seems to be an inherent character trait of most Japanese. Considering the still common marriage customs of the Japanese, this observance is more than casual and is not without foundation. Such being the case, arranged marriages are still very common throughout Japan and the go-between is still a factor in the life of many Japanese couples.

It is not a custom for young Japanese to seriously consider marriage at the early ages so common to life in the Western world. The young Japanese consider it more important to complete their education and to establish themselves in their business and professional careers before undertaking the responsibilities of married life. The emotions of love are not, many times, the major factors surrounding the decisions relative to marriage. Many Japanese, therefore, do not marry until they are in their middle or late twenties or even early thirties. The so-called Westernization of Japan has not affected this part of Japanese life as much as is often claimed.

As a young Japanese girl or Japanese boy reach the age at which their parents feel they should be considering a partner the parents begin to look for a likely candidate. In the case of a young Japanese girl her parents might handle the situation in the following manner.

In considering candidates for their daughter's hand in marriage the parents examine the backgrounds of likely males and discuss their feelings in this regard with the parents of the potential candidates. A go-between is selected whose job it is to get the two young people together. Pictures of the young people are given to the go-between and the job of arranging a date is begun. In separate meetings with the two young people

the go-between arranges a mutually agreeable meeting place and time. The go-between arms the two people with a picture of the other as well as their name and then sits back and hopes for the best.

The necessity for convenient meeting places has been the story behind the success and the proliferation of the Japanese coffeehouse. Coffeehouses in Japan are delightful to behold and for a small price the two candidates can dawdle and talk over a cup of coffee or tea for hours on end without disruption. It is not uncommon to see young people in public areas throughout Japan carrying a picture of someone while searching the faces of strangers in their midst. The eye identity is soon made and with halting hesitation a potential marriage is considered silently in the mind of each. Such meetings and resultant conversations are usually reserved and extremely polite considering the fact that the participants are well aware of the purpose for the meeting.

It is, of course, permissible for the young couple to meet more than once. They are, however, expected to make a decision rather rapidly and to linger in this matter is not considered appropriate as it casts bad vibrations on the parents and the go-between. The silent observers tend to feel that there is something wrong with one of the candidates which casts negative implications upon the parents of each. Should the union of the two not take place it is extremely embarrassing to the parents of the one who refuses the other.

Love is generally not considered to be a part of these initial proceedings, however, it is hoped that love will be a result in time to come. Obviously many marriages are the result and obviously many of them create life partnerships that exist without true love. Happily many realize love for each other and live out their lives in blissful happiness.

Within Japan itself the family unit is still a strong factor in the strength of the nation and the emotional and moral fiber of the individual. A young Japanese girl rarely considers living away from home until she marries. It is also true that most Japanese young men do not leave home until the time of marriage. In the case of the eldest son, it is his inherent responsibility to care for his parents for the remainder of their lives and so at the time of his marriage his new bride moves into the home of his parents.

Much of the Western world has, in recent years, experienced a deterioration of the strong family ties. Such liberation, as it is sometimes called, is not always healthy. While some facets of Japanese society are seeking to adopt more and more of the Western customs there is little in Japan to indicate a deterioration of the family unit in Japan's future.

17

Kampai

Max and Florence had concluded their tour of the sightseeing delights in Beppu and had left the sightseeing bus in the Ginza area. Ginza simply means *shopping district* and every Japanese city has its Ginza. Florence had wanted to ramble about the charming shops in the arcades she had seen from the bus earlier and Max had agreed reluctantly to join her on her shopping spree.

As Florence wandered about the shopping area with Max stumbling along behind in boredom, going in and out of every shop within reach, Max suddenly disappeared. Flo was, of course, preoccupied with her own little adventure and it was quite sometime before she realized that Max was no longer a part of her private tour.

Meanwhile, back along the shopping trail, Max had stumbled across a liquor shop, in front of which there was a row of old sake casks. He had noticed that a couple of Japanese workmen were leaning up against the sake casks having their own little party. The Japanese held their large bottle of sake aloft as if offering Max a drink and he readily joined them for a few belts of the Japanese national drink.

Sake (sometimes spelled *saki*) is the national drink of the Japanese. It is many times referred to as rice wine but is actually brewed like a beer. Historically the casks were used as the containers for sake, but in today's world it is bottled in extremely large glass containers from which the Japanese drink as Westerners do from a bottle of beer.

Kampai (*calm-pie*) is the most common toast in Japan and it literally means *bottoms-up* or *dry the cup* and it is considered an insult to your host not to act on the meaning of the toast. Obviously such behavior often leads to drunken frivolity and unsteady feet.

Sake is unique to Japan in its style and taste. It is made from large grain rice of the finest quality, has an extremely delicate taste and contains about 15 percent alcohol. It is traditionally poured from the large bottles into smaller ceramic or earthenware bottles and heated until quite hot. It is then served in small ceramic or earthenware cups and it is under these circumstances that the toast *kampai* comes into play.

The Japanese workingman, however, doesn't seem to care whether it is hot or cold and simply drinks it out of the original container with great enthusiasm. It was in such a situation that Florence found Max in a rather jovial mood not seeming to care whether she was there or not. With the sound of the word *kampai* ringing in her ears, she left the scene and grabbed a taxi for her hotel.

Alcoholics are not a common sight in Japan and alcoholism is not considered to be a serious problem. It seems that most Japanese have the ability to separate worktime and playtime into proper perspective and it is seldom that a Japanese lets drinking interfere with his work responsibility.

Sake is not the only alcoholic beverage popular to the Japanese as they also brew some very fine beers and produce grape wines of a rather high quality. They also produce a plum wine which is extremely good to the palate.

The Japanese also produce scotch-type whiskies in abundance. However, they prefer the imported whiskies which are extremely expensive when purchased in local liquor shops. A Westerner visiting Japan will be extremely well-received by friends and business associates if they come carrying gifts of imported whiskies and brandies.

Max somehow found his way back to the hotel from his little native street party and promptly sprawled across the bed to sleep soundly until morning. As morning came, Max found it somewhat difficult to relate the location of his head to the rest of his body and he finally realized the sneaky affects of drinking sake. Sitting in the middle of his hotel room he noticed one of the old sake casks and wondered how it had gotten there.

18

An Apple a Day

An apple a day keeps the teacher away according to the old rhyme that most of us learned as children. Many a cartoon has depicted a student giving his teacher an apple in hopes of getting a good grade or to aid in future relationships. Some visitors to Japan wonder what might be used to keep the students away as it seems that they are constantly running into large organized groups of students.

At first, tourists view the large groups of students as a deterrent to the enjoyment of their trip. However, it does not take them long to realize how orderly, friendly, and well-mannered these groups of students are and they often find their journeys enhanced by the friendliness and curiosity of the students.

In a country blessed with a total literacy rate of 99.5 percent of the population, education is quite obviously one of the most important aspects of growing up. The school system is very much similar to that of the United States of America comprising six years of elementary school, three years of junior high school, and three years of high school.

The Japanese like to think of their society as being

without social classes which in other lands is usually governed by the financial status of the family and its birthrights. In Japan, all students, whether in public or private schools are dressed neatly in uniforms representative of their particular school. The parents are required to supply and pay for the uniforms. Such a system places all students, in appearance at least, on an even and equal plane without discrimination.

It is a required part of the educational curriculum of every Japanese student to travel extensively throughout Japan during the 12 years of his or her education. This is done with caravans of buses, on trains, on ships in the Inland sea with accommodations provided in dormitories located throughout the country to house and feed the students. The parents must pay for these trips but the cost is minimal and at the end of a normal education a Japanese student has visited and studied his entire country firsthand. It is a beautiful system that makes a great deal of sense and explains the tremendous national pride as well as the self-pride of the Japanese.

It is amazing to observe the orderliness of these masses of students as they visit their country's historic points of interest. At first the visitor to Japan feels as though the students are staring at them. In actuality the visitor is more of a curiosity to the student than the student is to the visitor. Many of these traveling groups come from areas in Japan where foreigners are rarely seen and as a result they are tremendously interested in the behavior as well as the appearance of the foreigner. The English language is a required part of their education and they find themselves confronted with an opportunity to try out their ability.

Max and Flo, with their traveling group of Americans, had ended their visit to Beppu on the Island of Kyushu at the southern end of the Inland Sea. They were now riding aboard a Japanese train enroute to Hiroshima which was to be their next sightseeing stop. Max soon became restless and got up to take a walk through the train. Upon entering the next car forward he was literally mobbed by an entire car load of students, in uniform as usual, when they caught sight of him and his now famous oki onaka. He had been caught in a swarm of high school students from Hamamatsu on their way home after a study tour of the Island of Kyushu.

Max finally felt that he had to escape into the safety of his own car. As he did about six of the pretty girl students followed him back to his car and were delighted to find the group of Americans with whom they soon made friends. Soon the Americans found themselves receiving gifts from the students as tokens of their desired friendship. Most of the gifts were things that the students had purchased as souvenirs of their own trip. Some were to have been gifts to their younger brothers and sisters, or even to their parents. Somehow the students felt that they now wished to give these away and to refuse them would be a disaster.

The more time one spends in Japan the more conscious one becomes of the student groups. Feelings usually turn to warmth and respect for the students. Their behavior is impeccable. Their orderliness is regimental without actually being regimented. They all seem happy and jovial to the point of thorough enjoyment of their lives.

It is part of Japan. It is an intriguing sight for tourists to see students, the boys with their little uniform caps perched on their heads and showing shyness more than do the girls, orderly walking in a tightly closed group behind their teacher, and the girls with their smiling faces, dressed alike in middy blouses and pleated skirts, neat as a pin, their black, straight, mostly long hair bobbing and bouncing in unison as they giggle and smile shyly to those who observe. The openness of their faces and the brightness of their eyes does make the visitor to Japan feel welcome and warm.

Many visitors to Japan, in later recollections of their trip, remember most fondly their encounters with the students. To many an American lady a gift of friendship, innocence and sincere warmth has been shown when a pretty Japanese girl student shyly smiles and says what sounds like:

"Ha-row! You Ah-melican rady? How you rike Ja-pon?"

The adult population of Japan need not worry about the future leaders of their country. It is relatively certain that it will be in good hands.

19

It's Party Time

To many Westerners the mere mention of the word *Geisha* conjures up ideas of female entertainers not normally accepted in most Western societies. Max had no way of really knowing the functions of the geisha in Japanese traditional society and his senses were bursting with curiosity about this apparently acceptable form of feeding the male ego.

On their way by train to Kyoto, the American tourists had been told they would be treated to a sukiyaki dinner with geisha girls in attendance after they had arrived in Kyoto. Max didn't know quite how to handle this situation but it did intrigue him to say the least. Florence found herself wondering what she had gotten them both into and thought that maybe she would plead fugu fish poisoning for both of them and thus avoid the confrontation.

The custom of the geisha girl in Japan is centuries old and, contrary to some current information, is not passing from the scene of Japanese life. All centers of population have their geisha districts and it is not uncommon when in the Akasaka district of Tokyo to see rickshaw-like carriages transporting geisha girls to their evening assignment (a choice of words used

regularly by English-speaking Japanese). The rickshaw is covered in black and the geisha rides unseen by outsiders as she peers through a peep hole in her mobile tent pulled through the narrow streets of Tokyo. And also in Kyoto, the Gion district beckons with its wooden geisha houses and its red paper lanterns in preparedness for an evening of subtle female entertainment and convivial drinking and eating in studied companionship with some of Japan's most delightful female entertainers.

While it cannot be said that the Japanese housewives really accept this form of male chauvanism, it can be said that they have put up with it for centuries and for the most part it seems that they will continue to tolerate its existence. It is apparently something of a status symbol to most Japanese men to utilize the services of a geisha—which are seldom physical.

Over the centuries the geisha has become an aesthetic form of entertainment for those males whose wallets can afford it. To enjoy the company of a geisha, either at her geisha house or at a public restaurant is an expensive adventure to say the least. It takes years of training for a young girl to learn the many arts of being a geisha and most are devoted to the pursuit of their profession. Their profession involves learning their ritualistic forms of dress, the science (to them at least) of serving their male counterparts, the proficient playing of stringed Japanese instruments as well as the dances and games so much a part of a geisha party.

It was to such a party that the tourists were invited. While it is not normally customary for geisha girls or *maikos*, as the apprentice geishas are known, to perform in the presence of other women, it is rather common in this current world to hold such parties for visitors to Japan. Usually such parties require that the visitors wear *yukatas*, the light informal robe found in all Japanese hotel rooms as garb for relaxation. Such apparel relaxes inhibitions and adds to the frivolity of the occasion.

Max in a yukata was a sight to behold. His flowing robe cinched tightly by a sash, which also serves as a money belt, about his ponderous protuberance as if lifting it with pride and purpose. Florence, as would be expected, had her yukata wrapped left over right in the traditional manner of dead

Japanese ladies. Geishas aghast rushed to her assistance and swiftly returned her to the state of the living. Shoes were removed in good order and after much grunting and groaning they found themselves ensconced on the floor while confronted by the eye appealing array of sukiyaki ingredients about to be cooked to tender delights before their very eyes.

Max, with obvious pleasure, soon found himself between two very pretty Japanese bookends, geisha girls in personal abundance, each wishing to serve his needs for food and beverage. Florence was somewhat dismayed by this display, particularly since the girls did not seem to recognize the fact that she was even there or that Max was somehow important to her.

As the sake flowed in and out of its hot little cups and the beer foamed its way into the innards of the guests it became less and less important to understand the geisha and more and more important to appreciate her grace and beauty as she deftly and artistically did her job with graceful beauty and simple openness of purpose.

Most Westerners leave Japan not really wondering too much about the function of the geisha and choosing to remember her as a gracious hostess exemplifying the beauty and grace of Japanese life.

20

The Fortune Bookie

Our group of American tourists was on a sightseeing trip in Kyoto the very next morning and one of the stops included on the tour was a visit to the Heian Shrine and Garden. The shrine was a glorious display of the traditional orange and white buildings set around a courtyard of carefully raked white gravel, occasional well-manicured bushes and shrubs, and haphazardly placed rocks (planned to look that way). As with all gardens and landscaped areas in Japan, the Heian Shrine is a classic example of the informally formal simplicity so much a part of Japanese landscaping.

Max and Flo walked with their group of traveling companions through the courtyard which was teeming with bubbly, giggling kindergarten children on an outing with their teachers. The laughter of the children, the warmth of the radiant sun, and the beauty of their surroundings made Max and Flo both silently think that life was worth living. Many of the children were playing in the shade of a large tree nearby that seemed to be decorated with white slips of paper. Never before had they seen anything like this and they wondered at its significance.

Upon approaching one of the buildings of the shrine Max and Flo noticed considerable commotion at what appeared to be a souvenir counter on the porch of the building. An attendant, possibly a priest, was pulling some metal sticks from a brass cannister, reading something on the stick and then handing the purchaser an envelope.

"What is this?" they asked.

Their Japanese guide hastened to explain that the people were purchasing their fortunes from the priest. The guide hastened to add that the Japanese had a propensity for superstition and luck, whether good or bad, is considered a strong influence on their futures. Obviously fortunes purchased at a Shinto shrine or a Buddhist temple have extra sensitive implications.

Max and Flo both thought it would be fun to play the game and so they placed their bets with the fortune bookie. Each shook the brass cannister with vigor and after some difficulty extracted their personal metal sticks. These were handed to the attendant who carefully read the numbers on the sticks and after a search of the various little pigeon holes came up with an envelope for each of them. The fortunes were, of course, in Japanese. The Japanese guide eagerly offered to interpret them.

Flo's fortune went something like this as interpreted by the Japanese guide:

> Your appreciation of nature is a valued character trait. You must learn to relax or your health will diminish. A handsome, thin, dark-haired man is in your future. Now is the time for you to travel to foreign lands. Riches and jewels shall be yours for the asking.

Obviously she was delighted with her good fortune and Flo quickly put the slip of paper in her purse.

Max was eager to find out what his envelope contained and the Japanese guide interpreted the message:

> You miss much of the beauty of life in nature. Hard work will be necessary in the future. You will learn

to live without love. Now is not the best time for you to travel. Your financial problems will be solved in the future.

Max could not help but laugh and he silently wondered who had been the go-between in his marriage to Florence. The go-between had certainly not known how different they were.

The Japanese guide then told Max that when a bad fortune is received it is the custom in Japan to tie the piece of paper to a bush or tree near the shrine or temple with the hope that the spirits will forget the message. Rembering the tree under which the children were playing Max quickly took his fortune and tightly tied it around a small twig and silently hoped that it would be forgotten.

The Japanese are quite superstitious. You constantly hear reference to lucky and unlucky days and many a business venture is put off until a lucky day is at hand providing a welcome opportunity to consummate that important deal. Marriage ceremonies are seldom performed on unlucky days, however, on lucky days the hotels of every city are crowded with wedding parties.

Fortunes and fortune telling is serious business in Japan, but not with cookies—that's Chinese!

21

The Upside-Down Jellyfish

After their morning sightseeing tour in Kyoto most of our group of American tourists had resorted to shopping in Kyoto's quaint shops abundantly stocked with goods representative of Japan's arts and crafts. Max had, however, elected to leave Flo on her own and was pondering the results of his previous encounter with the fortune bookie as he sipped on a cold Japanese beer and watched a baseball game between the teams from Nagoya and Osaka on a nearby color television. The game made him feel that he was at home even as the Japanese umpire called the batter *out-o.*

As Max continued to watch the game he thought about the geisha party of the previous evening and in general indulged in thinking about the various aspects of Japanese life that he had now experienced. It was all really quite different and he found himself intrigued with the country and its people.

Max and Flo had accepted a proposal by their Japanese guide that they visit the Gion Corner in Kyoto to enjoy other samples of Japanese folk art, culture and theatrical arts such as the Bunrako puppets.

Later that evening Max and Flo joined other members of their tour group in walking through the narrow streets on their way to the Gion Corner. The streets were delightfully full of people scurrying to and fro with an occasional geisha being whisked to her next assignment in her mobile tent. The gay red lanterns of the geisha houses flickered their messages of identity as they laced the streets with color and danced in tune with the gentle breeze.

As they continued to walk through the little streets Max noticed that there was a preponderance of orchid colored signs, most of which included the symbol that looked like an upside-down jellyfish. Earlier in his travels he had noticed that this symbol was normally used on all signs that had to do with hot springs inns or massage parlors. He thought that all these signs certainly couldn't mean that all these places were hot springs or massage parlors and so he asked the Japanese guide what it all meant. An intriguing story that made a great deal of sense came forth.

The crowded living conditions of the Japanese are a widely discussed subject. The reasons for these conditions are obvious when one considers the density of the population and the availability of land area for housing purposes. Consequently the average Japanese family lives in considerably less space than does their Western counterpart. The rooms of a typical Japanese home or apartment are utilitarian and multi-purpose. A living room by day becomes a bedroom at night. A bedroom often shared by parents and children alike. Obviously this cramps the style of a Japanese husband in his love relationship at home. The physical aspects of life are rather open in Japan and most Japanese are rather uninhibited, but not quite that uninhibited. The curiosity of the children is sometimes a difficult thing to cope with and so the sign of the upside-down jellyfish is the Japanese husband's salvation.

The narrow side streets of all Japanese cities, towns and villages are dotted with the mostly orchid signs which frequently beckon customers to savor the delights to be found within the walls of these establishments. Many a lurid story is told about these quick-stop hotels as they are called. In reality the customers are, however, usually married couples seeking privacy from their families. These quick-stop hotels are luxuriously furnished and delightfully pleasant in atmosphere. They charge by the hour and their services often include gourmet food service in the privacy of the customer's own room.

Considering the delightfulness of these places and the logical purpose they serve in Japanese life, it is no wonder the Japanese government had to step in a few years back and encourage birth control. The quick-stop hotels are indeed an oasis away from the searching eyes, the giggling voices and the intuitive curiosity of the children. It all keeps peace in the family and peace in the land.

22

Throw-in Style

Max was in a quandry. "How can I get out of going to this," he thought to himself. He knew that when he got back home the boys would ask him what he had done on his trip to Japan and he just couldn't quite figure out how he was going to tell them that he had gone to a session on flower arranging. That just isn't the sort of thing a grown man is supposed to do in the mysterious Orient.

Ikebana, the art of flower arranging, is a part of Japanese cultural life and an integral part of the education of every Japanese girl. Due to their respect for nature brought about by their history of ancestor worship through the philosophy of Shintoism, the Japanese are meticulous as gardeners and apply to their homes a simple decorative style that compliments nature to its fullest. No self-respecting Japanese home would be without its garden and *ikebana* flower arrangements gracing its interior.

As with all Japanese arts and customs, the philosophy of respect, patience, tranquility and simplicity of purpose are utmost in the pursuit of these activities. Years of learning the arts of Japan as passed down over centuries of tradition instill

in the mind and the behavior of the Japanese a peacefulness in their daily lives that is not customarily found in many other ethnic groups.

The art of flower arranging is based on a rather simple principle involving a triad form in the presentation of beauties of nature—either flowers, weeds, grasses, twigs, stones, or large pieces of wood—arranged in simple containers. The three points of the triad represent heaven, man and earth in appropriate positions with man in the center. All forms of ikebana follow the same prescription in principle.

It was to such a demonstration of Japanese traditional folk art that Max reluctantly attended with Florence eagerly leading the way.

It was at this demonstration of the art of ikebana that Max found himself in the beguiling company of a young Buddhist priest who proceeded to perpetrate upon the restless males in the audience the principles of flower arranging while artfully maintaining his masculinity. The young priest was equally adept at feeding the palpitations of the female hearts as he adroitly snipped, clipped, flipped, and finally dipped in a graceful bow, displaying a beautifully balanced and simply arranged piece of natural art.

It now came time for the young priest to get someone in the audience to try their hand at ikebana and Florence quickly volunteered. Thinking of her marigolds back home she was quite confident that she could handle this task with dispatch.

Max was embarrassed for it seemed that compared to the arrangement the young priest had done Florence had created a floral abortion. He made such a fuss that Florence now wished she had a hole to crawl into and the young priest finally came to her rescue by getting Max on the little stage to do his own version of an ikebana arrangement.

One of the styles used in ikebana is commonly known as *throw-in style* and it was this style that the Buddhist priest now chose to demonstrate with the able assistance of Max.

In principle the throw-in style is supposed to represent the natural results of flower arranging with abandon and it was with abandon that Max proceeded to assist the young priest. Max was last seen lightly tripping (that's a little hard to imagine) across the stage carrying a large log which he was preparing to throw into a large wooden tub at the other side of the platform.

23

A Warm Chlorophyll Milkshake

A traditional part of Japanese social life is the tea ceremony. It is not religious in nature, even though Buddhist priests are often instructors in this cultural and social activity. It is not intended to be totally serious but rather is considered as a part of getting acquainted, as a formal introduction between new friends and as a graceful way of entering into the private home of Japanese.

After the adventure with ikebana demonstrations, Max and Florence moved into another large Japanese style room, simple in beauty, delicately scented with the aroma of fresh tatami mats. After the usual gymnastics of getting to the floor, not completely graceful and appropriate in their array, Max and Florence enthusiastically anticipated this new experience.

Off to one side of the room was a pretty Japanese girl, beautifully gowned in a kimono, preparing the ceremonial tea. Her movements were precise and it appeared that she was visually appreciating and enjoying the aesthetic beauty of the utensils she was using in the procedure at hand. A filigree of steam was rising from the cooking pot and the girl was deftly ladling the thick foamy green tea into large cups without handles to be distributed to the guests.

The same young Buddhist priest of ikebana fame was attending this ceremony and he proceeded to place one of the cups of green tea in front of each guest on a mat on the floor. A small sweet rested beside each cup and was to be taken to enhance the enjoyment of the tea itself.

As one lifts the large tea cup to drink from it, preceded with a bow to the host, one must hesitate to appreciate visually the tea cup and its artful appearance. Then the guest must turn the tea cup in his hand being careful never to touch the same part of the brim with his lips twice.

Max thought as he stared into the cup that the light green tea and its foamy hot head appeared not unlike "a warm chlorophyll milkshake." After he had tasted it he was not so sure that it didn't taste like a warm chlorophyll milkshake. It seldom is found pleasing to the taste buds of Westerners.

The tea ceremony is still an important part of social life in Japan. Every girl is taught the ceremony as part of her normal education and it is considered an extremely important aspect of social culture in the country. It is a delightful way to meet new friends as its simplicity tends to relax the inhibitions; it brings everyone together on a peaceful plane to encourage a warm friendship without animosities and hard feelings of any kind.

Such a custom could well be adopted by the political and governmental leaders of all of the world's nations as well as the general populace.

24

FLAT ON THE FLOOR

It was to be the last night in Japan for Max and Flo and they had decided that they would participate in a program called, "Meet the Japanese." It was a program that encouraged visitors to Japan to visit with a Japanese family in the privacy of their home. A car was being sent to pick them up at their hotel in Kyoto and soon the vehicle arrived driven by their host and his wife. Max and Flo were delighted to learn that their hosts spoke English very well and eagerly left in their company to enjoy an unforgettable evening.

It was quite obvious to Max and Flo that their hosts were not the average Japanese family and it was even more obvious when they arrived in front of their relatively large home on the outskirts of Kyoto. Max and Flo, of course, had to remove their shoes upon entering the house and Flo was intrigued to notice that it was the Japanese lady who helped them off with their coats. Unknown to them, the man of the house never does it, that is the custom in Japan.

In proper Japanese fashion a tea ceremony started the evening off. Considering that Max had not yet learned to love the warm chlorophyll milkshake it cannot be said that the

evening started off with a bang. The ceremony did relax natural tensions and the warmth of international friendship dominated the scene.

A tour of the house soon revealed that their hosts lived in typical Japanese fashion—on the floor. Not a chair was seen. Not a bed, Western style that is, was to be found. The doors all slid in grooves in the floor and the Japanese lady told them that Japanese superstition included the philosophy that to step on the grooves was to step on Buddha's head. This tale reminded them of the old game they had played at home as children in the United States when they avoided stepping on the cracks in the sidewalk.

Contrary to normal design in Western style houses it was noted that this house had the best rooms in the rear of the building. The lovely little garden was also in the rear, faced by a large picture window for convenient viewing. They had noticed upon entering the home that the front of the house seemed quite ordinary and little landscaping graced its small front yard. The beauty was to be found at the back of the Japanese house—a common custom in Japan.

Max and Flo had heard stories that the Japanese slept on the floor but expected this custom to have changed and that sleeping on the floor was no longer the regular way of life. They soon found this is not the case. Most Japanese still sleep in *futons* (Japanese style beds) on the floor. The tatami mat flooring of most Japanese homes is soft and luxuriant and provides a good base for the futon. The futon consists of a comforter style base with sheets and more comforters for covers. Most Japanese do use pillows, but they are extremely hard by Western standards. This explained the hard pillows Max and Flo had noticed were standard equipment in many Japanese hotels. Their Japanese lady host further explained that it is a daily ritual for the Japanese housewife to air her bedding in the sun thus providing a subtle atmosphere of fresh air and sunshine to a night of pleasant sleep.

Max and Flo had had a chance to sample the Japanese style of sleeping when they were in Beppu and now they wished they had taken advantage of that opportunity.

Their evening moved on with grace and beauty. Max and his male counterpart exchanged business cards and an invitation was extended for their hosts to visit them in the United States in the near future. The evening concluded with a short sightseeing drive through the residential areas of Kyoto and a drive through the grounds of a local university where their host was a professor in the English department.

It had been a truly delightful way to spend their last night in Japan. A country they had learned to love and a country to which they made plans to return.

25

Sayonara!

It is a fact of life that all things must come to an end whether
good or bad. So it is with Max and Florence and their
delightful meeting with the Japanese.

The last morning in Japan has come and in their Kyoto
hotel Max and Florence are packing.

Max is putting into his suitcase the ad from a Japanese
massage parlor that he never went to, a lock of hair from the
geisha girl's wig that he took secretly with his pocketknife, the
t-shirt he was wearing the first time a Japanese girl patted his
oki-onaka, a sake cup from the geisha party and, last but not
least, that sake cask he found the morning after in his hotel
room in Beppu.

Florence is packing towels from the various hotels she has
visited, a yukata emblazoned with the crest of the hotel in
Kyoto, a few ash trays from Japanese restaurants, a sewing kit
commandered from a hotel in Hakone National Park, slippers
from the hotel in Beppu, and on and on and on.

The Japanese don't quite understand the penchant that
many Westerners have for such souvenirs. Their pride is such
that they would never think of taking such souvenirs for them-

selves under any circumstances. It is really better not to be tempted in such a fashion—particularly when you are a visitor in another country.

At the airport Max and Florence are overburdened with their carry-on baggage and Max appears to be a peddler of sorts with flight bags hanging from both shoulders as he says goodbye to their Japanese girl guide and she gives him a friendly last pat on his ōki onaka.

Max and Florence have learned how to meet their Japanese friends in traditional style, they have had the shoes-off routine many times and are now experts at removing them. They have been swooshed, almost fugu-ed to death, geisha girled, massaged, kamikaze-ed in Tokyo and tea ceremonied in Kyoto. They have over indulged in food and beverage and they have danced the night away. Most of all they have learned something about another world, another culture, another set of traditions and now feel comfortable with the customs of another people.

Comfortably aboard the flight after takeoff, Max reaches into his flight bag and grabs a large *nijusēki nashi.*

What's a nijusēki nashi?

That's Max's secret. Why don't *you* go to Japan and find out for yourself?

PHOTO CREDITS

INDEX